Günter Gerngross · Herbert Puchta

PLAYWAY 1

PUPIL'S BOOK

Unit 1
Hello **2**

Unit 2
School **8**

Unit 3
Pets **12**

Unit 4
Having fun **18**

Units 1–4
Show what you can do **23**

Unit 5
Health **24**

Unit 6
Food **28**

Unit 7
Animals **32**

Units 5–7
Show what you can do **36**

Unit 1 Hello

1. Watch the story. Listen and stick in the pictures (CD/2). Sing the song (CD/3–4).

Unit 1

○

○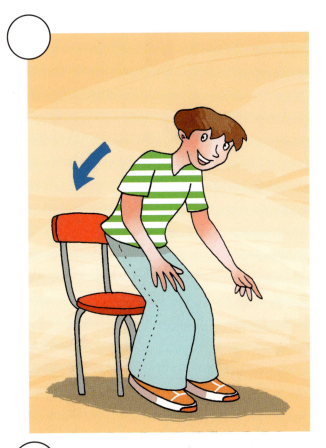

1

○

Listen and point. Fill in the numbers (CD/5).

3

Unit 1

③ Listen and point. Do the chant (CD/6–8).

④ Listen and point (CD/9). ⑤ Work in pairs. Look and speak.

Unit 1

6 Listen and colour (CD/10–11). Speak.

7 Colour and speak.

Unit 2 School

① Listen and point. Do the chant (CD/12–14).

Unit 2

○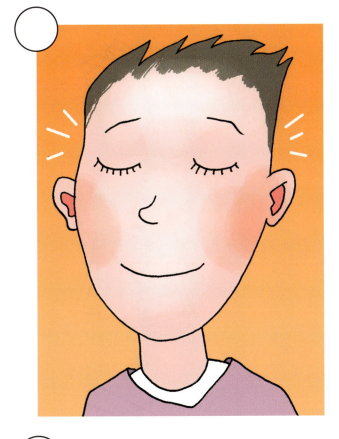

○

○

1

② Listen and point. Fill in the numbers (CD/15).

Unit 2

3 Colour and speak.

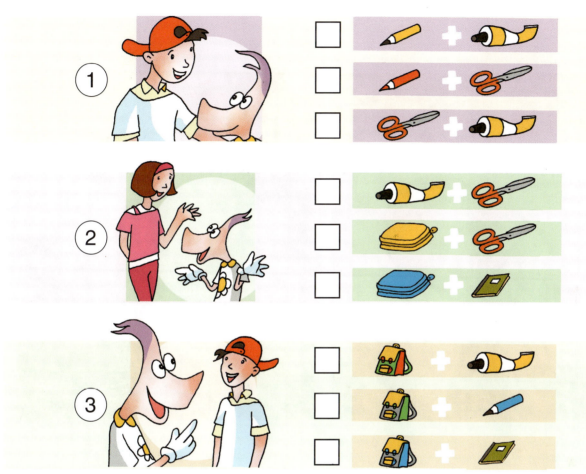

4 Listen and tick (CD/16). Speak. 5 Stick in the pictures. Work in pairs. Speak.

Unit 3 Pets

1

1. Watch the story. Listen and fill in the numbers (CD/17). Sing the song (CD/18–19).

12

❷ Listen and point (CD/20). Work in pairs.   ❸ Think and draw.

Unit 3

4 Watch the story. Listen and stick in the pictures (CD/21).

14

Unit 3

15

Unit 3

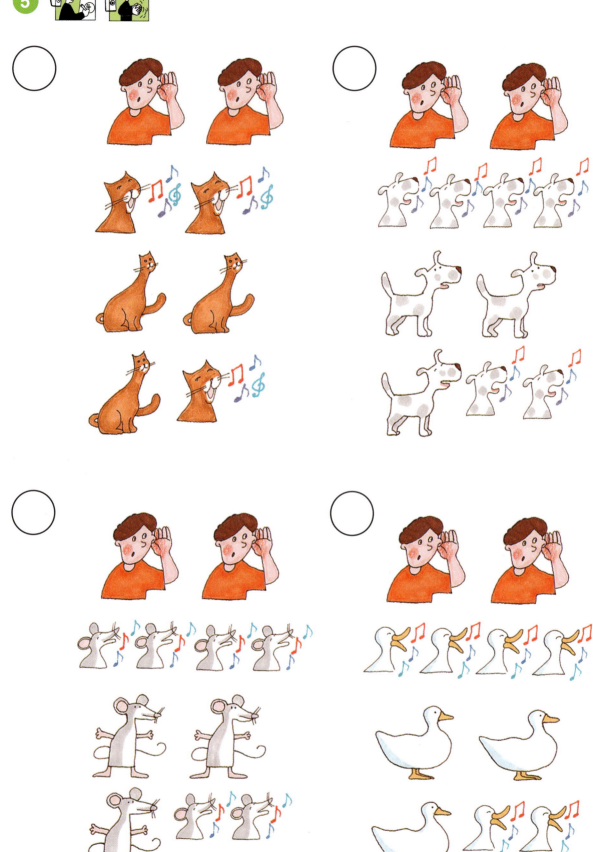

⑤ Listen and fill in the numbers. Do the chant (CD/22–24).

Unit 3

 Look and colour. Listen and point (CD/25).

17

Unit 4 — Having fun

❶ Listen and colour (CD/26–27). Speak. ❷ Colour and speak.

Unit 1 Hello

1

 Unit 2 School

5

 Unit 3 Pets

4

Unit 4
Having fun

4

 Unit 7
Animals

1

3 Listen and point. Sing the song (CD 1/28–29).

Unit 4

4 Watch the story. Listen and stick in the pictures (CD/30).

Unit 4

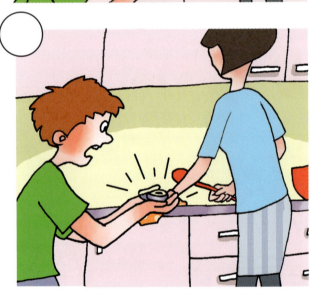

5 Listen and point. Fill in the numbers (CD/31).

Show what you can do

Units 1-4

1 Listen, take a colour and number (CD/32). Speak and colour.

Unit 5 Health

1

① Listen and point. Fill in the numbers (CD/33).

Unit 5

2 Listen and point. Sing the song (CD/34–35).

25

Unit 5

Watch the story. Listen and fill in the numbers (CD/36).

Unit 5

Listen and point (CD/37).

27

Unit 6 Food

① Listen and point. Do the chant (CD/38–40).

Listen and draw (CD/41). Speak.

Unit 6

Watch the story. Listen and fill in the numbers (CD/42).

 Listen and point. Fill in the numbers (CD/43).

31

Unit 7 Animals

① Watch the story. Listen and stick in the pictures (CD/44).

32

Unit 7

Unit 7

❷ Listen and point. Sing the song (CD/45–46).

Unit 7

Watch the story. Listen and fill in the numbers (CD/47).

35

Units 5-7

Show what you can do

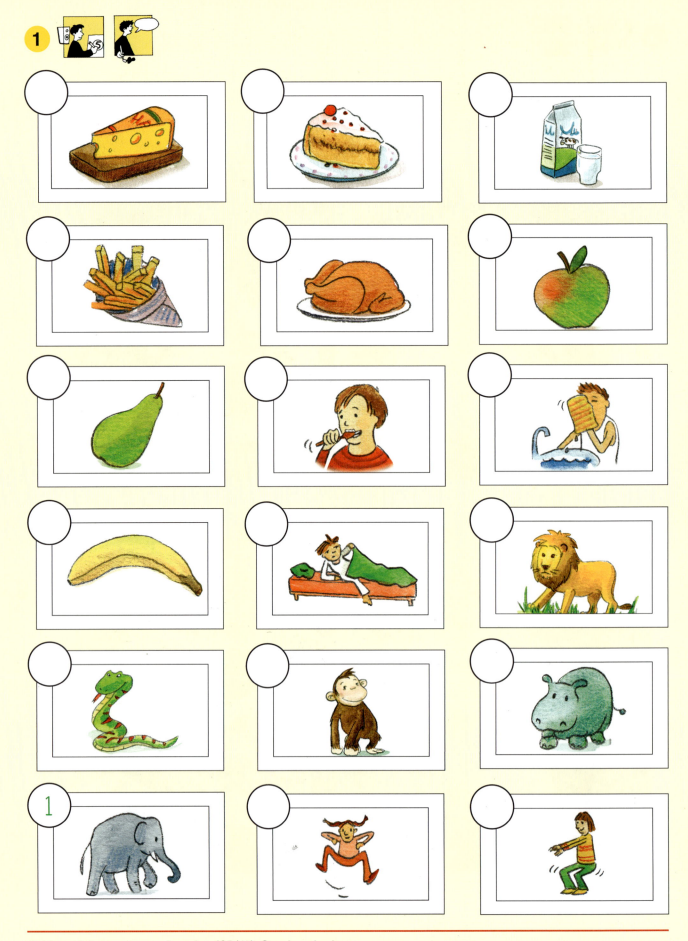

1 Listen, take a colour and number (CD/48). Speak and colour.

36